D0663170

The
Promised Land

The
Promised Land

poems

Philip S. Bryant

NODIN PRESS

Copyright © 2018 by Philip S. Bryant, all rights reserved. No portion of this book may be reproduced in any form without the written consent of Nodin Press except for purposes of review.

Some of these poems have previously appeared in *Water~Stone Review*, the *Blue Road Reader*, *North Dakota Quarterly*, and the anthology *There Is No Other Way to Speak*.

I would like to thank Norton Stillman, John Toren, and Nodin Press. And I'd especially like to thank Amy Eisenschenk for all her assistance and hard work.

Cover art: Allen Forrest. art-grafiken.blogspot.ca
Design: John Toren

ISBN: 978-1-947237-14-8

Library of Congress Number: 2018959337

Published by
Nodin Press
5114 Cedar Lake Road
Minneapolis, MN 55416
www.nodinpress.com

*To Renée
and my family*

Contents

here among them   the americans   this baffling
multi people   extremes and variegations   their
noise   restlessness   their almost frightening
energy   how best describe these aliens in my
reports to The Counselors

                       – Robert Hayden

Black writers see the Minnesota landscape
Differently, and because they are of this region
They see their world differently as well.

                       – Alexs Pate

All truths wait in all things

                       – Walt Whitman

I think something happened here;
I think this is the place where
deals were made, and angels held
their breaths in the sky above.

                       – Joyce Sutphen

I just want to do God's will. And He's allowed me to go up
to the mountain. And I've looked over. And I've seen the
Promised Land.

                       – Dr. Martin Luther King

The Promised Land

How Myths Begin

Last evening toward the very end of twilight, the sky
took the shape of a deep turquoise bowl, the outer rim
highlighted with burnt orange and red of the distant
horizon. I saw two pheasants run the length of a football
field across the plowed furrows. At first, they looked like
two small coyotes; I had recently heard coyotes laughing
late at night. They moved fast, two brown and golden blurs
racing across the tilled earth. All of a sudden, when I was
absolutely certain they were coyotes, they took flight and
arched high into the air over the highest treetops. That's
when I knew they weren't coyotes at all, but two pheasants.
Could they have been coyotes that somehow changed into
pheasants? Is this how myths begin? No way, I thought.
But late that night, right after I turned off my light, I lay
in bed and through the open window I could feel the cool
wind blowing in, like wings gently flapping. From out in
the dark fields came the faint sound of coyotes laughing.

GREAT CLOUD HERDS OVER SOUTH-CENTRAL MINNESOTA

For Nina Louise and Gabriel

Great vast cloud herds
Over south central Minnesota
Graze the high sky, late summer
Plateaus and pastures,
Along the bright sunlit
Dusty north August trails,
And cut through wide open
Swales and high windswept
Ranges, grazing and lazing
Under a rolling Texas-grade
Hill Country deep blue.
A thousand or so fluffy clouds
Lumber and shuffle southward
Along their way as we drive
Directly below them now.
And your sweet Grammie
Renée, a real farm girl herself
Born and raised, bets me as we
Watch these great cloud herds
Slowly move, that if we
Roll down all our windows
And are really, really quiet,
We could even hear them
Bellow and Moo!

A Complete History of the Blues in Just Six Lines

It wasn't all
That important
For white people
To ever listen to the Blues—
But it was important
For black people to sing them.

THE HALF-FINISHED REVOLUTION

The killing stopped at exactly four
The guns simply refused to shoot anymore

The long list of enemies burned hot and bright
No one was taken away in the middle of the night

No one manned the barricades at dawn
All the posters, pamphlets, leaflets were gone

The streets empty, the palace left unstormed
No fallen heroes, no martyrs to mourn

No one argued what was finally to be done
Kids played in the streets and simply had fun

Some ground had been bloodied but not much more
Not one single person signed up for the war

No grand pronouncements were ever made
About the radiant future or of a golden age

And everyone wondered if it had already been
It seemed to be over as it was about to begin

So maybe they thought it'd be okay
To put off history for just one more day

Both firing squads and condemned fell fast asleep,
So close to each other they could've danced cheek to cheek.

EMERGENCY POEM: BASED ON A CHILDHOOD MEMORY
FROM THE 1950S

This is just a test:
If this poem were an
Actual emergency
You'd be instructed
To immediately seek
Shelter in your basement
Or your cellar, go to a far
Corner, away from all
Windows, squat down
Low, put your head
Between your legs,
And kiss your ass goodbye!

THE CHRISTIAN SCIENTIST AND
CLIMATE CHANGE DENIER IN HELL

The devil asked the Christian Scientist
And the climate change denier
How they came to be in hell.
The Christian Scientist said for him
It was really hard to tell
It must have been an obvious
Error, that his name was placed on
The list, perhaps it was too hastily
Drawn, a typo, at most, he thought
A minor glitch. The devil nodded
Sympathetically and then turned
To the climate change denier
And asked the same question,
And the denier told the devil
There is no such error that I can
Rightly claim or readily boast,
So, you'll never believe me,
When I tell you, just last night,
My yacht hit this big-ass iceberg and
Sunk, right off the South Florida coast!

A Postcard from Chamberlain, South Dakota, July 2014

"White west is not Indian west" –Adrian C. Louis

I was their last customer of the day. They were just about to lock the door as I entered barely a minute before closing. I could clearly see the disappointment on their dark brown faces when they saw me coming, looking really hungry. They got almost annoyed and surely perturbed, not so much at me but at the thought of making yet another Subway sandwich at well going on ten o'clock as the bland white bread country music continued to play. It had been a long, hot day. Renée and I, on the other hand, had driven 600-plus miles with another 300 or more to go, and I was badly in need of a twelve-inch turkey sub with everything on it and a medium Coke to see me through further down the road. So here we were in Chamberlain, South Dakota, on the east bank of the mighty Missouri where Lewis and Clark paddled upstream on their way to make Manifest Destiny not just some murderous, half-baked nineteenth century political theory, but a hard, cold, American fact and reality. Now here it was—on a hot and dusty, late July night, two young bleary-eyed native boys were waiting on me at Subway. One, with a long single braid down his back, quickly stuffed iceberg lettuce, tomatoes, cucumbers, onions, pickles, yellow peppers on turkey and cheese with a thick line of white mayo squeezed out on top. "So, will that be all?" he curtly asked looking up again at the clock on the wall, speaking forced-sounding lines from a yellowed Hollywood western movie script. I just nodded, smiled a knowing smile that made him loosen up and relax a bit as I said, "Yeah, I guess that's it." I paid up and was set to go driving toward the great Corn Palace in Mitchell. What untainted possibilities and alluring promises Chamberlain offered after quitting time and was beckoning to those two young boys as they rushed to close, I would never know. Maybe some dark-haired beauty was waiting impatiently for one of them down by the riverside just on the edge of town. Certainly not the kind of promise Lewis and Clark once foresaw camped up here two centuries ago. They might be just a stone's throw away as this entire western plain must have seemed to be completely open to them on a similarly hot, windy, July day. This must not have looked back then so lost and godforsaken, but fresh and new and just ripe for the taking. Of course, it was not so for those who already lived here and called this their home, who already knew the sweet night-blooming scent of flowers by the riverside beckoning to them for perhaps a thousand years, long before there was Lewis and Clark or even the infamous Trail of Tears. A more sour scent hangs heavy, hugging close to the ground as we started driving east out of town into those haunted, late evening, interstate hours, into the suddenly chilled Dakota air that fills with the scent of those night-blooming flowers spreading out over this land, everywhere.

EVANGELINE'S, AUSTIN, TEXAS, 10:30PM,
OCT. 26th, 2016

Late night
Blues club,
White guy
Blows harp
Outlines
The knife's
Edge
Still
Razor
Sharp!

NAZIS 2.0

Like any red-blooded American
Boy growing up
In the 1950's
I was told to
Simply hate and loathe Nazis
But the other night
Holding Polynesian restaurant-style torch lights
There they were
On the march once again
Looking clean shaven with
Strangely matching boy band haircuts
Dressed in white J. Crew polo shirts
And neatly pleated
Non-wrinkle khaki pants
Of cotton-polyester blend
These guys, minus the jack boots,
death's head insignia
German Luger, dueling scars
And monocle
sure didn't
Look like Nazis
I feared and hated
So much in the 1950's
Or the horrors
I remembered seeing
Early on when
Our parents let my sister
Shaun and me
Stay up late and watch
Night and Fog
Yet, here they are, updated and reloaded,
Still marching in single file

Still shouting their all
Too familiar "*Seig Heil.*"
Rebooted jackboots, marching
Einsatzgruppen 2.0
Maybe these sorry motherfuckers
Thought with their new
Abercrombie and Fitch blazers
And Sperry topsider boat shoes
Nobody would ever remember,
Who they really were, or even know

THUS, KNELT COLIN

And on the far, far, sidelines,
During our national anthem,
Thus, knelt Colin,
Head bowed down
To the ground
As if in some deep,
Silent, mournful prayer,
Long before anybody
Noticed him,
And long before
Anybody else dared.

The Promised Land

No lie, this really happened:
Renée, Elizabeth, and I were driving
To Charleston and stopped late
At night in Rocky Mount, North Carolina,
Off I-95 and found a Hampton
Inn there because Renée likes
The feel of Hampton Inn's laundered
And pressed bedcovers and sheets
The mattresses firm yet pillow-soft,
A contradiction, I know, but still
True. We were feeling or maybe
It was just me feeling a little
Skittish about us, a mixed-race
Family traveling in the deep South,
Those old horror stories I heard
Growing up in Chicago running through
My head like grainy yellow flickering
Film clips of *Birth of a Nation*.
And boy, checking in at 12:40 AM
And hearing the deep Dixie-dipped,
Stars and Bars, bleach blonde accent
Of the night manager as she asked,
"Ya'll come here from very far tonight?"
"Yes," I said, we'd come far without saying
Really *how* far. She just smiled, told us
"Ya'll have a real good night now," what was
Left of it. In the morning I put my fear
Aside and went downstairs for the
Complimentary coffee and breakfast
Which like the beds were quite excellent.
The small dining area was packed to
The gills with people of all hues, shapes,

And colors. Brown, yellow, red, black, white,
Christians, Muslims, Hindus, Jews,
All quietly sipping black coffee, eating
Biscuits, grits and gravy, country ham,
Scrambled eggs, cereal, fruit, cream cheese
And bagels, and those waffles you can make
Yourself from a mix poured onto a sizzling
Hot waffle iron. It looked like dining
Area of the United Nations.
Very conservative, southern white business
Men mixed with newly-arrived immigrants
Speaking Mandarin in the far corner
Behind a racially-mixed family tending to
Three light brown, beautiful cherubs.
Their thin, white Grandma Clampitt herself
Helped them as they ate their bowls of
Fruit Loops and drank little cups of orange juice.
Overhead a big flat screen TV loomed,
Flashing the latest doings at the Trayvon
Martin murder trial, yet people would only
Glance up at it for a moment then turn away
Going back to their coffee, muffins or family.
I stood up with my two cups of dark roast
Coffee to take back to our room, but I didn't
Want to leave. I wanted this beautiful sunny
Morning in the southern half of our country
To last forever, even though in an hour or two
Renée, Liz, and I would have to be on the road
Driving farther south toward Fayetteville,
Spartanburg and east into Charleston. As I'll
Never hope to say it like Dr. King once said it,
That I somehow climbed a mountain top in my life

And saw the promised land, nor can I say
Without a doubt that I firmly believe that we
As a people will ever get to that promised land,
But in Rocky Mount, North Carolina, one warm
June morning in the small dining area of the
Hampton Inn off I-95, for a brief moment
I saw something that at one point in the
Violent and tragic history of this country might
Never have been even foretold, as I glanced at the clock
And had to go. With Charleston almost six hours
Away, Renée, Liz, and I had to quickly
Pack up our van and hit the road.

DANCE TOO?

> *"I am born to be lonely, I am best so!"*
> — *William Carlos Williams*

When the kids are sleeping
Count all two of them,
Hers a boy, six, and hers
A girl, seven, and their cats
Asleep by some big over-stuffed
Chair by the bookcase downstairs,
The two of them living together
In some small dusty town
Stuck out in the middle of
Nowhere, say in southern
Minnesota, say just outside
Of Faribault or Zumbrota,
And there it all begins
In cold, misty, early spring
Just above these mottled and
Muddy country roads, where
Shitty boot prints from the barn
Are left on every living thing
The truth be told, there in the
North room they dance naked
Together, admiring each other's
Arms, faces, flanks, buttocks,
Set against the two "yellow drawn
Shades" now pressed closer to
Each other as they bend and sway
Just the two of them dancing
To ward off the spring chill
And cold, and who shall say
They, too, are not the happy
Geniuses of their household?

THE MAIN DOWNTOWN CHICAGO POST OFFICE IN THE 1950'S

In the 1950's, I remember
People would often joke
That the main downtown
Chicago post office
Was just the
South loop
Branch of the
University of Chicago.
Of all those mail handlers
And sorters down there
Almost all of them had
Their BAs, MAs, or PhDs,
And all of them, mostly black,
Now, just imagine that!

To a Warm African Sun

For Paschal

Dropping Renée off at
The heating plant parking lot
Up on campus for her morning
Spanish class, I see one of my
most esteemed colleagues and my
old friend from the Modern
Languages and Literature Department
Paschal Kyiiripou Kyoore
Dressed in beautiful handwoven
Traditional all white garb from
Ghana, perhaps its Dagara.
(I must ask him later)
As I drive past I honk and wave,
He turns and smiles a smile
As big and as warm as a midday
African sun and waves back
At me, I think quite regally,
Like I imagine an African prince
Or perhaps even a king once
A very long time ago
Might have done.

LONELY SMALL-TOWN STREETS

I will arise and go now, out onto the lonely streets of this
small white town. And on most days, I'm the only black
person I see walking around. But there, just walking up
ahead I see a lone dark figure steadily walking nearer,
a young black man dressed in a black t-shirt and black
oversized baggy pants. His black hair is in neatly braided
cornrows that fall gently down his shoulders. As we walk
past and nod in assent to each other, I notice now that
he looks much older and wonder then if he is thinking
the same thing as me. As we quickly pass, our eyes briefly
meet, and without a single word to each other we seem to
speak about two black men walking all alone, seemingly so
far from home, down these lonely small town streets.

MALCOLM X AT TEMPLE NO. 2: CHICAGO 1960

Malcolm stood before
The cheering throng,
Pointing to Elijah,
Bejeweled fez on his head.
"This is your prophet;
This man is the embodiment
Of the truth of almighty Allah."
Elijah sat erect, his eyes
Seemingly fixed on some
Dark spot on the far horizon.
Malcolm had turned smiling
Toward the crowd again
As applause and cheers
For him and not Elijah
Grew into an even more
Fevered pitch. Directly
Behind Malcolm, the other
Ministers began to notice
That the prophet seemed
To be looking at something
Off in the far distance
Too small to see with
just the naked eye.
But taking the shape
of something slender
And sharp going in
Like a small prick from a pin
Felt suddenly on the skin
Before the blood
Came rising
to the surface.

THE GREAT BLACK MIGRATION PROSE POEM

Now this prose poem suddenly showed up early one Saturday morning. I hear a gentle but steady tap at our back door. I open up the door to a whole family of my long lost southern cousins with their eight kids in tow and more. They look like they just stepped off a train from the deep south, the old country, to Chicago circa 1936 —part of the great black migration no doubt from the horrors and killing poverty of the deep south. They carry with them all that they own in rugged, battered suitcases tied together with twine. All wear what looked like their Sunday clothes—thread-worn and tattered but clean, neatly pressed, trying still after miles of hard traveling to look their best. And I'm puzzled, I ask them do you know where you are and what year it is? The train you took seemed to have missed Chicago by about 400 miles and by about 80-odd years. They all look momentarily startled and then one of my cousins nods and says that indeed may be so. But still could I please put them all up for a few days, they'll try not to be a big bother to me though. If you can spare us some bed and board and something to eat until me and the missus here can get back on our feet. Who am I to refuse my own kin as I open the door up wide then as I welcome them in. Renée puts on a pot of red beans and rice, cornbread, okra, and ham hocks, as we sit down at our dining room table, and before we all partake, my cousin bows his head and in this slow southern drawl, he says grace. He gives thanks to the good lord for the food and for us and hopes they don't cause us too much fuss. Almost nine decades of migrating from the Deep South to up north—to get away from the terror and the fear. I dare not ask why it took them this long to get up here, or why they overshot

Chicago by almost 400 miles and now somehow landed in Saint Peter, Minnesota, after 80-some years. As they all quietly ate, Renée and I could only marvel at them in total awe at their great migration and meditated on how far and wide these long lost relatives of mine straight from Bow Junction, Arkansas, along with this prose poem, so like us all, had to wander and roam to get to a place that any poem like this one could feel really welcomed, even loved and wanted, and then could maybe even start to call this cold, icy, northern outpost, home.

ADAM & EVE

Like Adam and Eve,
we once played so free
in the fallen leaves
in a cold late autumn breeze
as a deep darkness fell over
our quiet empty street.
Let's go someplace,
she said to me, where no one
will see.
And she took me by the hand
down that narrow leaf-strewn pavement
and down into her dark secluded basement
where I dared to show her "mine"
and she dared to show me "hers"
until we heard someone
unlock the door outside and call for us
suddenly guilty of what we had done,
stood terrified there
in her dark basement
for a long, long time
as she soon covered up what was hers
and I then covered up what was mine.
And for a long time,
couldn't look each other directly in the eye
for what we did nor answer the reason why.
So long ago now,
it's only for those cold fall days to know
why we played so free
like Adam and Eve
in the fallen leaves in a cold late autumn breeze
as a sad deep darkness fell over
our quiet empty streets

in that far ago distant time
what was on our minds
when she dared show me hers,
and I dared to show her mine.

A Little Spanish-Speaking Island

The other day on the south end of town a group of
young Latinos barreled up in a bright red extended
cab Ford pickup truck with a Dallas Cowboys star logo
stuck on the left rear bumper and Texas license plates.
They all got out of the rear extended cab, yawning and
stretching their legs, smiling and all speaking rapidly in
Spanish. And suddenly the cold Minnesota March wind
blew just a bit warmer, the sun got brighter and in the air
was the smell of freshly made tortillas, offerings of dark
micheladas poured in tall, frosted glasses, refried beans,
pears, oranges, guitars, brass marching bands, illuminated
paintings and statues of Our Lady of Guadalupe and
strings of multicolored lights forming big, wide-toothy
grins across these dark, drab buildings and streets. All
at once in the dirty, crusted and melting snow I felt so
warm and tropical and smiled at one of the boys who
glared at first but then smiled and nodded back to me—
now on our little Spanish-speaking island off the coast
of Mazatlán— yet surrounded by cold northern ice and
snow and the rest of these small town people standing
around us who had *also* heard these warm, lovely, musical
sounds but could not feel the warmth that had traveled
all this way north and could not seem to thaw their icy
frowns.

Groovin' in Grove City

Drove through this quiet little town
Didn't see a single soul around
Groovin' in Grove City

West on US-12, she said
When I met her last night on the web
Groovin' in Grove City

She looks so soft and round
Built straight up from the ground
Groovin' in Grove City

Passed the Garden of Eatin'
Passed Hoggin' the Road
Groovin' in Grove City

Couldn't take my rest
Till I found that sweet mama's address
Groovin' in Grove City

Drove up and down those streets
Asked everyone there I'd meet
Groovin' in Grove City

But they all said the same
Nobody ever heard of that name
Groovin' in Grove City

So sorry to have driven that far
Thinking, man, what a damn fool you are
Groovin' in Grove City

But all these houses here look so sad
When you surely know you've just been had
Groovin' in Grove City

Such a one-horse town
When the sun goes all the way down
Groovin' in Grove City

Big semis zoom by
And man, it almost makes you wanna cry
Groovin' in Grove City

Past the Garden of Eatin'
Past Hoggin' the Road
Groovin' in Grove City

Now I paid my dues
Got these Meeker County Blues
Groovin' in Grove City

Went and wrecked my happy home
Now I'm out here all alone
Groovin' in Grove City

Yet, could it be
She's still out there waiting for me
Groovin' in Grove City

As I drove slowly out of town
I saw not a single soul around
Groovin' in Grove City

SMILE

For Alexs Pate

There just across Madison and Third street
recently arrived immigrants, a young
mother and her two children, a girl
and a boy, with tight-rung curls of jet
black hair like sparse patches of thick
shrubbery on some arid desert plain.
I look at them and smile. The boy with
curly spools of black hair, looks back
at me and smiles, and I think of all
those thousands of miles they had
to travel to come here to this very cold
and often lonely, godforsaken place
where the deep brown of his round face
can easily break into a great big
smile all the way from Somalia, East Africa,
a true smile just for me and for all those who
pass by him now, who don't even look,
or maybe choose not to see.

BELL RINGER

Black Lives Matter
As all lives *should* matter
You *could* say
Both are just different
Parts of the same thing;
Yet, a bell will always need
A bell ringer, you know,
In order to ring.

HOMAGE TO POOR RICHARD

Alas, poor Richard
my uncle,
now long gone
and while still alive
so up against it
during his
short, sad life
a great
unsung
US Army cook
I was told
in his day, but
got piss drunk
one Christmas Eve
in Korea, 1951
the year of
my birth
court marshalled
and possibly
discharged quite
dishonorably for
falling asleep
and letting one
hundred
Air-lifted
Government-issued
Turkeys burn
to a crisp
that were
supposed
to be for one
Big feast on

Christmas Day,
For our hungry
homesick
frostbitten
troops
to feast and partake,
and believe it or not
my uncle wasn't shot,
"real racial progress"
back then, I'm sure,
they thought.
Alas, poor Richard,
I speak you fair
in death,
Remembering
the black cast-
iron skillet
cornbread
You used to
make when
I was just
three or four
years of age
so, soft, supple, all
Around, it rose up
from the very depths
of something sweet,
And golden brown.
It was pure Southern honey
dipped right from heaven
Lovingly sliced, as if
portioned out from

a Mississippi Delta sun
That shone warm and bright
That at least for a
brief moment
chased all
those dark storm
clouds of your
short, sad, life,
far away.
I still remember how near
your skillet cornbread
was to perfect.
As the sweetest taste
of it still lingers
in my mouth to this day.

WAVE

Once years ago, I was on
a tour bus, somewhere
deep in the Mississippi Delta,
we stopped in this tiny,
little town, it was very hot,
early summer and it looked
like not a single soul was
around, I remember some
tourist who had to get off
got off and after a bit, the
ones who had to get back on,
got back on. The streets were
still empty, quiet, still, all around
as the bus started to slowly
pull out of town and suddenly
there on the side of the road,
stood a tall gaunt black man,
looking to me, about 80, or
maybe even 90 years old,
waving to us as our tour
bus went on by, and I
think there wasn't a single
soul on that bus who knew
the reason why, and sadly
it's a fact, no one on that
bus ever waved back,
it seemed to me that they
didn't really want to know,
if the whole truth be told,
why some old black man
in the Mississippi Delta,
waves to them from

the side of the road,
perhaps it was just
him waving goodbye,
as our tour bus, surely
didn't stop to find
out or ask him,
as it drove on by.

BLUE TRAIN

For Carolyn Marie Wilkins

Blue train at the station
Blue train on the track
Blue train blows that whistle
Like it ain't never coming back

Blue train cross into Georgia
Blue train deep in Tennessee
Blue train in Alabama
Blue as an eye can ever see

Blue train all across the country
Blue train over the sea
Blue train got hold of my baby
Blue train got hold of me

Blue train round the mountain
Blue train here in this town
All aboard says the conductor
This blue train's freedom bound

Blue train shines its blue light
Blue train shines its red
Blue train shines a green light
on all that open track,
straight up ahead

Blue train way up north
Blue train deep down south
Blue train cross that Mason-Dixon
And you all know what train I'm talkin' 'bout

Blue train round 'bout midnight
Blue train right before dawn
Blue train got my baby
Who done packed her bags and gone

Blue train make me holler
Blue train make me shout
Blue train rattle my windows
Blue train shook my house

Blue train got my body
Blue train got my soul
Blue train cross that trestle
And don't never wanna let me go

Blue train in the cotton
Blue train in the corn
Blue train makes me wonder
Why on earth I was ever born

Blue train you hear me talkin'
Blue train passed on by
Blue train blows that whistle
So lonesome, it makes me cry

Blue train in my song
Blue train on my mind
Blue train here an' gone
Blue train all down that line

Blue train in the morning
Blue train late at night
Blue train left the station
Blue train out of sight

Blue train round the mountain
Blue train right here in town
All aboard said the conductor
This blue train's glory bound!

PEACHES AND CREAM

For Shaun Alexis

Seemingly out of nowhere, I
Remember our Grandfather Hampton's
All-time favorite ice cream,
Peaches and Cream,
So, Shaun, was it Wanzer Milk Company
Back in the 1950s that made it, or
Was it Sealtest or Borden's, I can't
Remember which. Maybe it was
The time we were at our Bow Junction,
Arkansas, cousin's tiny farm
Outside the town of Covert,
Michigan, when they cooked up a big
Batch of southern fried chicken.
Just a few short hours before,
That great big platter of golden brown,
Perfectly fried chicken had been walking
Around pecking random bits of seed
And corn from off the ground.
This was before the Colonel, Popeye's,
Church's, or even Harold's Famous
Fried Chicken were ever around. There was
Corn bread, macaroni and cheese, bacon
Grease slowly simmered with fresh-picked
Pole beans. And afterwards, for desert, we
Had our cousin's homemade ice cream.
Remember, you and I turned the crank
Of that old-fashioned oakwood bucket
Ice cream maker, turning and churning
For hours on end. Our cousin even gave us
A silver half dollar, real money
In those days, to keep the crank going.

The ice and salt around cream and
Home-cooked custard, flowing.
I seriously thought my arm was going
To fall off, but just when it seemed
Turning the crank was way too hard,
Our cousin appeared, smiling, with a
Big bowl of sliced peaches picked
That morning from her small orchard.
The turning was all downhill then and it became
A soft, luscious peach and cream blend.
We churned and turned until all those
Fresh slices of peaches were churned all the
Way in. For the topper, our cousin
Scooped that peaches and cream ice cream
Right over a freshly baked slice of her peach
Cobbler still warm out of the oven. Then I
Remember our Grandfather Hampton, who
Had worked so hard with just an eighth grade
Education to support his entire family,
Since he'd been age eleven, how he took just
A spoonful of the cobbler and peaches and
Cream ice cream from his bowl, lifted
His head right up to the skies, and proclaimed,
"This has got to be heaven!" He was a man
Of few words, always quiet and reserved,
But we watched his eyes fill up with tears
Of pure joy and happiness—*glisten*—
I remember just as it was then! When
Grandfather Hampton spoke
We all looked up from our bowls of
Peaches and cream ice cream
And listened.

It was my senior year of high school. It was a late
Sunday afternoon. I was actually doing my homework
assignment for Monday. It was early April and it wasn't
for certain whether or not I would finish all my school
work on time with passing grades to graduate. Suddenly
out of the blue, one of my erstwhile girlfriends, a white
working-class girl from Marquette Park, (considered by
blacks off limits and enemy territory then) who loved
literature and William Blake as much as I, and who I
met at the main downtown branch of the public library
where she worked, was now calling me like a fair damsel
in distress. She and a friend of hers (another white girl
who had dropped some bad acid earlier in the day) were
downtown on the verge of freaking out, and needed
somebody sober to walk around with them and gently
bring them down from their bad trip so they wouldn't
wind up doing something stupid like try to jump off the
Michigan Avenue Bridge and fly down the Chicago River
because they thought they'd "suddenly sprouted wings
like angel-headed hipsters" or something. I still thought
of myself as chivalrous and even courtly in those days—a
black proletariat Don Quixote—so instead of dueling
windmills on horseback I promptly charged downtown
on the Jackson Park/Englewood "El" to talk down my
lovely, enchanted Dulcinea and friend from their bad
acid trip. In my pocket, a Modern Library hardback
edition of the *Selected Poems* of William Blake she had
given me as a birthday present. Upon meeting them at
the Wabash entrance of Roosevelt University they were
happy and quite relieved to see me. I could clearly see the
"tombstones in their eyes" to quote from "The Pusher,"
an old Steppenwolf tune from way back then. As we

walked north on Wabash with the thundering "El" passing over us, I read out loud poems from *Songs of Innocence and Experience* to quell the chemically induced storm that raged inside them. And I wished I could have raised my magic staff that rolled away that psychedelic haze like Prospero as he reassured Miranda, "Be not amazed child, no harm done!" And indeed as we walked they did become less agitated and more calm. So I kept reading Blake out loud to them. The streets were completely deserted so there was no one to witness this very strange and curious sight of a young black boy from the South Side reading William Blake aloud to these two stoned-out white girls who were tripping on bad acid. But out of those poems' powerful sounds they both slowly began to come down. We sat and rested in an empty newspaper and magazine kiosk on Washington Street and Wabash. I'm reading away—more Blake—when suddenly I noticed the sky has somehow darkened quite a bit as if night has instantly come, lightning fast, and when I looked up I saw we were completely surrounded by six to eight of the biggest, blackest members of the Black P. Stone Rangers, the most notorious and murderous street gang in Chicago then. I ceased my impromptu poetry reading as one of them breaks into this big, toothy and quite sinister grin and says jovially, "Brother, we decided we can't let you have both these white girls for yourself, that'd be greedy we think on your part, so you're going to have to share and give one of 'em up to us, so which one is it going to be?" All of a sudden I think of Black Panther founder Hughie Newton's famous revolutionary decree—whether I'm going to be part of the problem or part of the solution—only now I get to choose which way it's going to be. So can I be as wise as Solomon who, presented with the baby claimed by

two mothers, drew a sword to cut the child in two so
each mother can share an equal half? Or like the movie
Lifeboat, have my two little high white girls draw straws
and the shorter one, chosen fair, go with those blood
red beret-wearing P. Stone Rangers to only god knows
where? And indeed the devil in me was shouting from my
left shoulder right into my ear, "Let 'em take Dulcinea's
friend, you fool, being she's definitely not the looker
Dulcinea is!" But in this deep bottomless pit of darkness,
I see a tiny sliver of light shine through. I catch one of
the stone-faced Rangers' attention and look straight into
his eyes. He has not said anything one way or the other
and I immediately know he's their leader. I go directly
up to him and make my most impassioned appeal, and
humblest of petitions. I simply tell him these sad white
girls are tripping on bad acid and I was trying to bring
them down by walking with them here, downtown.
And as we all stood in the center of that deserted, cold
kiosk, I asked if he could find it in his heart for these
poor, helpless, white girls and myself to grant us some
small measure of mercy and pity. He stood and looked
at me for what seemed like centuries, then looked at the
pale girls trembling in terror like thin discolored leaves
just about to be ripped by some terrible gale from the
tree. He motioned to all his homeboys to move on and
leave us alone. Without any protest or hesitation they
did exactly what they were told. I thanked him again and
again, and he just nodded and said "Don't worry about
it man, I understand," and that was it. As overhead the
"El" continued to roar and thunder past the place where
to this day, I still believe it's no small wonder why pure
grace was offered and then received. Like a twelfth-hour

pardon or reprieve, or just a temporary stay of execution mind you, but call it what you may, perhaps as William Blake would simply say:

"To mercy, pity, peace, and love
All pray in their distress;
And to these virtues of delight
Return their thankfulness."

ASTRAL TRAVELING IN ELBURN, ILLINOIS, DURING THE EARLY 1970'S

Oh Dave, right now
I'm playing Pharoah
Saunders' classic Impulse
Album *Thimbe*,
"Astral Traveling" and then
"Red, Black, and Green,"
and I just imagine you
still very much alive
Back in the day
in the early 1970's
Stuck out in Elburn, Illinois,
Your big bay window in your
Book-lined writing studio
Wide open, smoking your corn cob pipe
gazing at the first dandelion of the season
on a clear warm sunny spring day
"Red, Black and Green"
Blasting away on your stereo
Pharoah on his tenor sax
in that calm late-afternoon hour
pours out black faith,
black love,
black hope,
black power,
all into the quiet streets
of your small, mostly white,
backwater town. Almost all your
neighbors covering their ears
and wondering what planet were you from
and how could you even know there exists
in this world such a sound?

THIS IS THE SEASON

Last night it was so cloudy and cold out
But the distant stars, it seems, were
Cut down to size for once and
Placed by Ben, our son, so lovingly
Around a small tree in our backyard.
There, a whole constellation shone
In the shape of Orion
And now burns through the night.
For this is the season, the stars
Can crown bare tree branches
And a young boy can clasp
A single star in his mittened
Hand and string those starry
Lights far out across
This dark, frozen land.

After Bathing at Baxter's

You came and offered me a flower
I was still awake, and the only one up
at that ungodly hour
After bathing at Baxter's

I still smelled a little hint of your must
and heavy patchouli oil scent
After bathing at Baxter's

You gave all your possessions away,
and hitchhiked all alone out to LA
After bathing at Baxter's

We didn't know a thing about love,
so checked off "all of the above"
After bathing at Baxter's

Tell me who was to blame for the whole world
then was still fightin' about that same thing
After bathing at Baxter's

Mushrooms dropped, looking out for the cops
After bathing at Baxter's

We saw Jorma jammed with Jack,
so white, blonde and young they were
But you know, I still was going to be black, even
After bathing at Baxter's

We saw Jimi play the Mississippi Delta Blues,
didn't think we had to pay those kinds of heavy dues
After bathing at Baxter's

We dressed so red, white, and blue,
That buckskin fringe jacket was me,
and that thin see-through Indian sari was you
After bathing at Baxter's

1968, armored personnel carriers rolled down my block
Neither of us would ever make it back to Woodstock
After bathing at Baxter's

I can't remember now if your name was Martha
or were you crazy Miranda who just lived
her whole life on propaganda
After bathing at Baxter's

We had no other plans, other than to dry hump for hours
and then just maybe kick out those jams
After bathing at Baxter's

Our world then was teetering on disaster
Or more like a nuclear war just the day
After bathing at Baxter's

We believed we were the crown of creation
in a racist, white supremacist nation
After bathing at Baxter's

We crashed at your funky little pad
you lit sandalwood incense but it still smelled pretty bad
After bathing at Baxter's

Having those young girl Sunday blues
way back then was all a poor white girl could ever do
After bathing at Baxter's

We didn't really know if we were the problem
or whether we were the solution
depending on which day or what revolution, before
Or After bathing at Baxter's

We were at a concert in the rain all stripped down
scrubbed and washed each other clean,
MLK still had his dream
After bathing at Baxter's

I had a dream you were still in the streets,
panhandling spare change, still dressed in tatters
and this was years and years
After bathing at Baxter's

But I remember you came and offered me a flower
when we were the only ones still awake
at that ungodly hour
After bathing at Baxter's

EATING WONTON NOODLES WITH LANGSTON HUGHES IN GUANGDONG PROVINCE

For Weiyi Lu

Right now, on the other side
Of the planet, I imagine
Langston Hughes somewhere,
Deep in Guangdong Province,
Slurping down savory Wonton
Noodles, cooked steaming hot
In fresh vegetable broth,
Laughing out loud at himself
As he tries to eat for the very
First time with chopsticks,
As everyone there around him
Laughs and slurps noodles as well,
Yet it's very hard for me to tell,
That deep into Guangdong Province,
Located way on the other side
Of the planet, who, there, other
Than me or maybe you, would ever
Think to imagine slurping steaming
Hot Wonton Noodles and Snow Fungus
Soup, laughing and eating with none
Other than the great, black American
Poet himself, Langston Hughes!

November Blues

Finally, all the air
Is let out of the balloon
As flakes of snow
Will be flying soon
And all that's left
Of our glorious fall
Is piled under leaves
Blown cold and raw
And now the sky
Is cloudy and gray
And there's not much left
For us to say
On this chilly, windy, November day
As things from now on
Will grow darker and colder
All the cake has been eaten,
And the party is over.
So pull on your coat,
Mittens and gloves
And hold on tight
To the one that you love
For all the air has gone
Out of the balloon
And flakes of snow
Will be falling soon.

The Thread

In memory of Jeffery Rosoff

Look, the very thin thread
Of our life is still there—
Though it's almost
Invisible to us now,
So wind-swept, loose
It blows through the air
Where often times a leaf
Can be blown farther
Than any of us can see—
Yet the thread remains,
Unbroken,
Somehow,
Stretching
Into eternity.

MY FIRST MUSE

She tore up all my poems
I'd written her just the week before
And threw the tatters and shreds
Of notebook paper where I'd
Carefully copied them out
To scatter across the classroom floor,
This dark beautiful south side girl
Whom I remember I thought I loved
More than anyone else I had ever
Loved in the whole wide world.
"Nigga' please! Are you kidding me?
Why you even bother to give me these?
I hate to hurt your
feelings, but your poems are the
last thing that I need in my life. If
you had a car, some decent clothes
and some money, I might think
you giving me these was cute
and maybe even funny. But you know,
as the old tune goes, if you ain't
got no money, then you sho' ain't
getting no honey, plain and simple,
because in this world, it ain't no joke
to be stone broke, if you hear what I'm
saying? I don't mean to hurt your
feelings, but when I read your
poems, I thought, 'Really, is you a faggot?
Fuck, are you really serious?' I told myself,
'If he really wants to talk to me, at least
He'd show me some car, some clothes
Or some money.' Now you tell me,
What the hell I'm going do with all

Your Goddamn poetry?" She laughed,
And looked straight at me full of scorn
And also just a little pity. And then she
picked up her schoolbooks and curtly
Walked away, having said, I suppose,
What she felt she had to say. I learned
something vitally important about art
and life that day, as I slowly stooped
to gather up all my heartfelt poems
She'd just shredded and then scattered.
She spoke the hard, unvarnished truth,
A gift she gave me, a feckless, clueless youth,
Unswerving in her merciless brutality.
I felt so beat up, hurt and battered,
But when everything was on the line
She took the time to show me that
What a poem says and doesn't say, at least
Back in those days, still really mattered.

SWITCHBLADE KNIFE

It suddenly sprung up
From somewhere deep
Inside its beautiful ivory
enameled fold
A sleek 7-inch razor-sharp
Stiletto, a brand-new blade
That my uncle, a sometimes
Street hood and on-again,
Off-again junkie, gave me,
strictly on the QT,
whispering don't let
your mother ever see.
So, in bed late at night
I flicked the tight-wound
Spring and slid my finger
Along the razor's edge
Of that sharp, deadly knife,
Immediately, repeatedly,
Thrust and stabbed
Well into those dark
Unsettled late night hours,
Pictured cutting into
Soft, pliable flesh as easily
As cutting the stems off
A fresh bouquet of blood
Red flowers, I stabbed
And slashed the stifling
Hot summer air, at whatever
In the dark, I imagined a real
And present danger to me
Hidden there, and for the first
Time in my young and still

Untested life, I felt not a bit weak,
Timid, or scared, as I, so cock sure,
Manish and bold, flicked the sharp
Cutting blade back into its fold.
Feeling just ever so guilty
Maybe even criminal, like I didn't
Have to try and be a very good
Boy ever again, truth be told,
So just before the first morning
Light, straight into the garbage can
Out in our back alleyway I tossed
That knife and as if on cue came a
gust of wind off the lake, that
Strangely blew, for the midsummer
Season very icy and very cold,
Beckoning from those distant remote very
Wild regions I suppose, just as a little voice then
Whispered from deep inside, pleading for me not to go.

A *Mighty Fortress is Our Trane*: Reported to be Heard Sung from a Passing Slave Ship, July 4th 1776 (Though This Date Can't be Fully Verified)

Dedicated to my nephew, Patrick Idries

"A mighty fortress is our Trane
A bulwark never failing
Our helper he amid the flood
of mortal ills prevailing:
for still our ancient foe
doth seek to work us woe;
his craft and power are great, and yet
When blessed by *A Love Supreme, A love supreme,*
Trane's power here on earth is more than his equal!"

BLUE MONK

In Memory of Dave Etter (1928-2015)

Blue Monk
Blue funk
Blue skies
Blue lives
Blue seas
Blue trees
Blue breeze
Blue me
Blue lights
Blue nights
Blue birds
Blue words
Blue train
Blue rain
Blue laws
Blue balls
Blue cars
Blue Bars
Blue tears
Blue years
Blue smiles
Blue Miles
Blue coats
Blue notes
Blue gloves
Blue loves
Blue shoes
Blue moods
Blue days
Blue haze
Blue roads

Blue modes
Blue moons
Blue rooms
Blue tones
Blue moans
Blue signs
Blue times
Blue States
Blue plates
Blue books
Blue looks
Blue kites
Blue flights
Blue wails
Blue tales
Blue beats
Blue streets
Blue waves
Blue Dave
Blue bog
Blue fog
Blue mounds
Blue frowns
Blue towns
Blue sounds
Blue funk
Blue Monk.

Beating that Boy

Love, imagine all my lies
As just a small frightened boy
Who always tried to run and hide
From his raging father and one day,
Belt in hand, called him out
To be a man and come
And take his proper medicine.
Look at him huddled there
In terror and in fear
Hidden deep in someone's dark closet
As his father flings open the door
Letting in the bright light of day
Shining in on that dark place
He tries in vain to hide in.
Listen how that small boy hollers
And tries to run for cover
As he's caught and dragged out and
Takes the first hard blow of the belt,
Trying as best as he can to protect himself
As he howls a little like Old Yeller did
Near death wracked with pain,
So too cringes and cowers
As it seems his father will beat him
Like a dog for hours and hours
As he pleads and lies that it wasn't him
Who committed that crime or awful sin
Which only makes his father
Bend his belt down on him even harder,
Determined now to dig out and uncover his lie
Buried deep down in the root
To beat this small frightened boy
Until he finally tells him the truth.

Racing Through This Beautiful Life of Ours

I spot this very large brown and white
Hawk perched high atop
A tree, and for miles and miles
Around I imagine he can now
Clearly see, perched above
Busy Highway 169, just as
Renée and I drive past, and I
Think does he ever wonder as
He watches all these cars zooming by,
Why we humans choose to race
Through this often beautiful
Life of ours, so damned fast?

ICE VOTIVE

Out in our backyard
Renée's ice votive
She molded from an old
Plastic paint bucket and
Filled with frozen tap
Water, steadily
Shines through the night,
In the very cold,
Bleak stillness
Of a Minnesota winter,
There now appears
This one Flickering light.

EMPIRE OF SNOW

More snow falling
On top of snow
That I remember now
Falling almost a whole year ago.
Barely has this winter begun
When another Empire of Snow
Falls on top of and completely buries
The previous one.
So in its cold, swirling white-out
Gyre, a blizzard arises
A whole Peloponnesian Empire,
Then a Greek Empire,
Followed by the Holy Roman Empire,
The Austro-Hungarian Empire,
The German Empire,
The British Empire,
All somewhere now buried deep down below
So quiet and frozen
All mix into one
Where they lie
As one roaring blizzard after another
Comes year after year
As way up here this season
Always turns out to be a bitch!
As many winters later
No one can ever tell
Which one was which,
As they all seem to blend and drift into the other
All through our falls, winters, springs, and summers
Rising and falling
As they come and they go.
These now great lost Empires of Snow.

THE WAFFLING SEASON

I fear my love
thaws and freezes
thaws and freezes
like the bare snowless ground
now made so barren from
this flip-floppy season.
Over and over
it advances and then ceases
when it can't decide,
be it young or be it older
on wanting to be ever milder
or forever colder.
I hope in March
when the metal spikes
are driven into cold hard bark,
maple sap will freely flow
From the lukewarm heart
so sweet and plentiful
and the waffling season
and love of mine
will finally choose and make up its mind
and its constant turning finally ceases
filling buckets of its sweetest harvest
from all that it now
thaws and then freezes.

LIKE A PRAYER

For L. Owen

Early last evening
I watched a white Sandhill
crane fly directly overhead
I looked up at it
and carefully took aim
in its direction
with all my best
thoughts of the day
checking first
to make sure
it was perfectly lined
up in my sights
before it flew away,
yet neither a sharp
arrow nor a well placed
bullet I shot
but only one or two
good, warm thoughts
lighter than air
to be mumbled softly
as if all alone in a
dark, empty church
like a prayer,
or taking a last-second shot,
where I hope my aim
was true, and hit its mark,
as I watched that
beautiful crane fly
off and disappear
into the dark.

A LITTLE RAIN, WIND, AND SUN

For Eleanore Fish

A sudden gust
Of strong wind
Brings a hail
Of these pale
Brown helicopter
Seeds, sailing down
From high up
In the trees,
Whirling their
Scythe-like blades
Round and round
In the air—
Harmless enough,
They cut and slash
All that lay in their path,
Devil may care.
Yet it's a peaceful
Airborne invasion
You'll come to see,
Bent on planting
Just a few of these
Small precious seeds
For a time that's
Still yet to come,
A quiet, all the way
Nonviolent revolution,
That makes this world
Greener, better,
With just a little
Rain, wind, and sun.

THE OTHER WAY AROUND

Sometimes it's enough just
To sit here for hours and hours
And watch all Renée's wilted
Burned out, summer flowers,
All these faded golden-yellow
Leaves that fall one by one, falling
From these almost stripped bare trees
And look back on all of time then,
130-billion years and counting
at what's now already been,
and all that water flowed under
the bridge, So what kind of
message to us do you think time
really sends? At night, a distant flicker
of starlight, like us, both new
and old, free floating photons on
some constant stream of a
seemingly never-ending flow.
When I glance up at these distant stars,
Do I dare think they glance back down at me?
Or it could possibly be just the other way around,
I like the Prodigal Son, once lost and now is found,
Destined to return back home, from my long journey,
That to all my loved ones, waiting there to greet me,
must seem to them now like it's taken me, almost an
eternity.

Thirteen Short Yellow-headed Blackbird Songs

1.

This yellow-headed
Blackbird
Looks way better
Than photos in a book.

2.

Glued to their phones
They miss this
Yellow-headed blackbird
Already flown.

3.

A bright yellow bolt
Of lightning
Struck the head of
This blackbird, dead on.

4.

Yellow-headed blackbirds
And red-winged blackbirds
Fly under their own flags.

5.

Red-winged common to find
Yellow-headed
Nae only spotted one,
this time.

6.

The strange song Nae heard
Turned out to be
The rare yellow-headed blackbird.

7.

I'm blessed to see
this one yellow-headed
Blackbird fly,
Before I die.

8.

Without uttering a word
I pray
to the yellow-headed
Blackbird.

9.

Yellow-headed blackbird—
A bright morning sun
Lifted up on black wings.

10.

This yellow-headed blackbird
waited an eternity
Just to be.

11.

Thanks to Nae
I came to see,
a yellow-headed blackbird
In our tree.

12.

Yellow-headed blackbirds
If nothing else,
Pure poems
Unto themselves.

13.

Yellow-headed blackbird's
Flown and gone
Somewhere deeper
Into this song.

SOS

Biking past a pond up on campus
On a warm spring evening
I hear hundreds of croaking frogs
Agitated, alarmed seeming, as if
Belching out a series of gruff S-O-S
Distress calls that come straight from the
Doomed, sinking, *Titanic* itself, foretelling
Of terrible things soon to come our way,
As they croak their frog S-O-S to us all day, right here
In River City, croaking loud and clear so that to
Casual passersby, perhaps if they could understand
Frog a little better, it would certainly alarm them now,
And all these dire warnings, shake them up somehow,
Down to their very foundations, so it be abundantly clear
When these frogs croak their last S-O-S, they even now
Barely can hear.

A LOVE SUPREME, FIFTY YEARS TO THE DAY
FEBRUARY 26TH, 2015, SAINT PETER, MINNESOTA

You made it this far dear John, all this time even up to
these frigid and arctic climes, with icicles hanging from the
trees, as someone somewhere begs and pleads, 'Baby can't
you hear me moan and cry to let me into your kitchen
cause it's gonna be rainin' outside.' Snowing and sleeting,
in our case, along with a red, flushed, numb, frostbitten
face. But even through all this you still appear, after rock,
disco, punk, alternative, rap, and hip hop and fifty-odd
years, you gently knock on our back door, and I say please
come in, come in, Trane, Elvin, Jimmy, and McCoy. All
looking so young and in still their prime—after all this
time, not one of them gotten old. Come in, come in and
warm yourselves gentlemen from the driving wind and icy
cold. And after a bit of Renée's good Minnesota home
cooking, you set up your instruments to play, only after
asking us if it's okay. Okay? I shout! Are you kidding me?
Play on dusk till dawn, I say, through the long cold lonely
night and day. Without any doubt Trane, you still know
what life's essentially all about. After many long years they
all suddenly appeared as if all of them just stepped straight
out of a passage of "I Have a Dream." Trane gently taps
out the time on our kitchen table and then softly chants
the opening chorus of "A Love Supreme"…
A love supreme,
A love supreme,
A love supreme!

JAZZ HOUND

"Where's your Dizzy, Where's Clifford Brown?"
                                    – Dave Etter

I'm just a jazz hound
Singing the blues
In this small southern
Minnesota town
A long way from home
So throw this dog a bone
'Cause I'll always need the *big beat*
And something hot and greasy
To eat, or just a little scrap
Off your dinner table please
A little Bird, Prez, Diz, or Trane
Dexter Gordon, George Cables
Or even a glass of Muddy Waters
If you're able. I'll never be
A real rube or hick and you
Can't really teach an old dog
New tricks, so just hand me
My "Goodbye Pork Pie Hat,"
Because "Now's the Time"
To "Better Get Hit in Yo' Soul"
And listen more closely
To the "Fables of Faubus"
And by the way
Can you tell?
I really do dig Charles Mingus
And I do love Modern Jazz
Even if they do on occasions
Play it too darn fast
As I do believe what
Howlin' Wolf once told

My high school buddy Rodney
And me, he said, "Boys, they'll
Always be, at least in this country
Enough damning incriminating
Evidence and irrefutable proof
That the blues ain't nothing
But the low down dirty truth."
So put on some Lady Day,
Bean, Duke, Art, or Monk
And you'll see that this
Old dog still can hunt
'Cause even up here
In the cold white north
I can still faintly hear
Old Reverend Dippermouth
Holdin' forth
Getting down, blowing all
Those high funky notes
And soulful, down-home sounds
Even way out here
In this lost Swede town
So please give this dog a bone
'Cause he's a long way from home
Just doggin' around
Still hunting after all these years
For the hippest bossiest sounds
Just like some old jazz hound
Still payin' dues, still singin' these
Lonesome down-home blues
The bluest and funkiest to be found
Right here in this lost Swede Town.

At the Bird Island Broaster

The Bird Island Broaster
Hands down, best fried chicken around
The Bird Island Broaster
Right off Highway #212 on Main Street
In this sleepy little town
The Bird Island Broaster
Years ago, Rez and I stopped there for lunch
The Bird Island Broaster
For no good reason, I guess Rez just had a hunch
The Bird Island Broaster
When Rez and me walked inside
The Bird Island Broaster
It smelled just like we walked
in some fried chicken joint
on the Chicago South Side
The Bird Island Broaster
Floured and buttermilked, piece by piece
The Bird Island Broaster
I then knew them Lutheran church basement
ladies were cooking with grease
At the Bird Island Broaster
Of course, I ordered my chicken all dark
and then Rez ordered his all white
The Bird Island Broaster
But that wide-hipped good-looking waitress
Just smiled and winked at us
And said it was all right
The Bird Island Broaster
I could be right, or I could be wrong
The Bird Island Broaster
It was just like I got a letter from home
The Bird Island Broaster

Rez and I were so happy,
we left that waitress a real big tip
At the Bird Island Broaster
As she walked away from our table
She gave us each a little extra shake of her big wide hips
At the Bird Island Broaster
So now Philip, you say they make the best fried chicken
At the Bird Island Broaster
Like they had a bunch of southern, black
church women cooking in their kitchen
At the Bird Island Broaster
Yet, if the real truth were ever to be known
The Bird Island Broaster
You can come way up north,
and find yourself right back down home
At The Bird Island Broaster
Rez and I stopped there once for lunch
The Bird Island Broaster
'Cause Rez I guess just had a hunch
About the Bird Island Broaster
I imagine best southern fried chicken for miles around
at the Bird Island Broaster
Out there in the middle of nowhere
Cooking that good fried chicken
in some lost Swede town.

A Red-Headed Woodpecker Signals Spring

A red-headed woodpecker
Taps on cold, hard
Tree bark, and makes
These faint flickers of
This Morse Cold
Spring suddenly spark
Short dots, long dashes,
That can transmit cold
White embers or the last
Smoldering ashes of
A slowly dying winter.
This woodpecker taps
To finally signal spring,
Too far off somewhere
Beyond these snow
Packed fields to bring
Tender young roots,
Small delicate fruits,
Plump, plentiful seed,
Soft green leaves or
A warm spring breeze,
Long before spring
Has ever begun
He signals for them to
Come, as sure and as
Fast he taps to them now,
As their little feet can run!

YEAH, YEAH, YEAH ! ! !

For John & James Cha

I'm so old now I can remember when the Beatles first
came to America, watching them on the Ed Sullivan
Show that fateful, frigid, February night. The next day it
seemed, the whole world was transformed and every white
kid in the country had grown their hair long and was
reborn. They combed their hair straight down over their
eyes loudly proclaiming,

> *She loves you Yeah, Yeah, Yeah*
> *She Loves you yeah, yeah, yeah*
> *She loves you yeah, yeah, yeah, yeah!*

Screaming it and shouting it up to the skies. They
knew the Fab Four had for them finally unlocked that
heretofore chained and locked door. For us on the
South Side of Chicago another door, marked only for
us, opened the same way, a few days after the arrival of
the Beatles. Kicked down really, by this brash, trash-
talking loudmouth black boy from Louisville, Kentucky,
who would then "shock the world" as he liked to put it,
again and again and again. I felt and heard that shock
for myself, crouched on the floor of my grandparent's
kitchen, listening to the first Liston-Clay heavyweight
fight on their radio. My family all gathered there, stared
at each other in complete and utter disbelief—Clay in
their minds was supposed to get pulverized and absolutely
creamed, though we couldn't hear or see young Cassius
at that very moment, celebrating and dancing around
the ring, shouting, "I shocked the world! I shocked the
world!" over and over again.

The very next day, instead of trying to comb our very
nappy hair forward over our eyes, not that we could have
back then, even if we tried, I remember us practicing
our version of what Clay would later call his Ali Shuffle.
Picture 11 and 12-year-old, skinny, knock-kneed tawny
black boys, me and all my long-lost boyhood friends,
knowing for certain that cloudy afternoon, our world was
never going to be the same ever again, as we jabbed and
danced, bobbed and weaved, more like modern ballet
than boxing, with all our new-found grace and ease.
We thought we literally floated like butterflies, and yet,
of course, stung like bees— "Yeah, yeah, yeah!" as we
shadow-boxed all afternoon, I remember we'd shout.
My best friend, pretending he was Clay (soon-to-be Ali)
would throw a blurry flurry of sharp, crisp combination
punches at me, pretending to be Liston, as he bobbed
and weaved, in and out, replaying over and over again
that mythic bout. We knew our chained and locked door
was now kicked wide open and our world had suddenly
changed forever, and I remember, we loved him, *yeah,
yeah, yeah,* without any doubt.

SIXTEEN-INCH CHICAGO-STYLE SOFTBALL
IN THE LATE 1950'S

Years, no decades now ago, on a
Hot, sweltering July night on the
South Side of Chicago, at
Meyering Park, across the
Street from St. Columbanus
Catholic Church, between
South Parkway, now Martin Luther King Drive,
And Calumet Avenue, just south
Of 71st, I saw really large
Fat black men,
Playing sixteen-inch Chicago-style softball
For the Skyway Tavern
With garish, loose fitting, black
And red and green softball jerseys,
Under the smoky fuzzy lights of the
Chicago Park District
One very big, fat black man
Stepped up to the plate,
The hour then for
Us kids, I remember,
Was way past our bedtimes and so
Very, very late, take one mighty swing
of the bat and lift a big sixteen-inch Chicago-style softball
High into the dark misty Chicago
Sky, way above the lights
And far above what else I can remember of
That late 1950's night,
Literally,
Launched towards the deepest
Part of outer space
It looked

To us kids then pretty clear
That ball was rocketing somewhere
To the very edge of the earth's
Outer atmosphere
Before Sputnik, Yurie Gragarin, Mercury,
Apollo, Gemini, or one small step for man,
And one giant step for mankind,
Way above those park district lights
That sixteen-inch Chicago-style softball
Took its fateful and historic flight

As I remember, us kids stood
And looked up and watched that ball fly
In complete awe and wonder
And from a far distance in the sky
We heard the dim drumbeat
Of midsummer night's thunder
As that really big fat black man
From the Skyway Tavern
Slowly circled the bases,
And from the hushed and stunned crowd
Rose not a single murmur or sound
As we silently watched and bet
If that softball he just hit
Would ever come down
Or, on a sweltering hot midsummer night
Perhaps sixty or more years later
I can gaze up at these very same heavens
And from afar
See it still there
Shining dimly still,
Steadily climbing, all sixteen inches of it
Ascending like some newly discovered planet or star.

WINTERFEST IN ST PETER

The other night working late in my office up at the college, I
heard the thud, thud, thud, and the boom, boom, boom, of
our annual Winterfest fireworks display and ran down the quiet
empty hallway to the big, north-facing window in Vickner
Hall to see the bursting, blooming red, green, yellow, flowers
of sound and light—a bright colorful and expertly arranged
bouquet and all, breaking into full bloom on this cold winter
night, celebrating in the depths of one of the coldest, bleakest
winters we've had now in a number of years. A winter that
comes complete with plenty of ice and snow and of course
the requisite amount of sub-zero, Arctic cold. So celebrating
our winter festival could be akin to Napoleon exiled on
Elba, celebrating the defeat of his once great and seemingly
invincible army at Waterloo or Londoners launching fireworks
to celebrate the introduction of the Black Plague to their fair
city back in 1665. It's an odd thing our Winterfest for sure,
but no odder per chance than celebrating Guy Fawkes Day in
England or Bastille Day in France—though we have no scary
wooden gallows to show, thank God, or guillotines on display,
only semi-naked, slightly inebriated, northern European white
people who will tomorrow take the "polar plunge" into a
nearby icy reservoir, all in good fun. But even these bright
colorful flowers of light that now explode and then completely
vanish out of sight and only briefly illuminate this long cold
winter night, yet are at the core, I think of any short-lived and
quickly fading delight, that can easily be all our slim chances
and hopes we all toss up into this frigid wind, just hoping
against hope it will all turn out better for us, somehow, in
the end. As I'm sure someone in a jet plane flying overhead
right now will look down from 30,000 feet and see from
that great height our tiny bombs and shells bursting bright,
through this long winter night and perhaps think of all the

God awful weather we certainly must endure living here, most of the year, and how truly wretched is this bleak, cold climate—as they shiver and watch our colorful, now waning, fireworks display and wonder what in God's name do those poor people way down there possibly have to celebrate?

LITTLE GRAY SQUIRREL

I just saw a little gray squirrel
jump from my neighbor's roof
to an adjacent tree
gilding high through the air
almost effortlessly, in free flight
and so graceful, taking his chances
he flew and then landed quite safely
on some high thin birch tree branches.

No human I know
Could ever perform such
A rare, death-defying feat, no matter how much
we proclaim our sovereignty and our reign
over the entire earth, and all of its beasts.

A LITTLE SPRING SCRIBBLE

For RLR

Love, doesn't
This warm spring
Breeze stir you
Just a little, or maybe
Do these few words
To you that I now
Scribble—
Look, those
Dry fallen leaves
Buried and trapped
All winter long
Under the snow
Are now blown free
To travel
In whichever direction
This warm breeze
May blow, .
Wherever it may
Take them,
They'll go,
Much like these
Words to you
That I now scribble,
Or this warm
Spring breeze
That I hope
Still stirs you too,
Just a little.

The Green Canoe

Early one morning on my way back from dropping the kids off at school I see a rusted out Dodge mini-van turning onto Broadway headed east across the bridge that spans the Minnesota River, strapped on the roof is a green canoe. Suddenly I think this guy must have just called in sick— told his boss he had this terrible stomach bug that was such a fright and kept him up half the night and he was so sorry to say, that he just couldn't make it in today. Then made his early getaway out of town, to one of the many small, well-hidden, outlying lakes nestled in the surrounding hills between here and Le Center and beyond. As I imagine him now sliding the green canoe into the water, splashing into it, paddling out onto the waves, with not a single soul around—only light rain and cool wind and waves hitting the smooth hull of his green canoe; his paddling making the only sound. As he takes a deep breath and slowly exhales and thinks of all the poor bastards he left now slaving hard at work, as if a convict successfully broken out of jail. He can hear them pissing and moaning as the machines they work at are constantly grinding and droning, as he feels that bittersweet guilt of the escaped convict suddenly rising up from somewhere deep underneath the waves, and maybe it's enough to carry him and his green canoe today, right to freedom's edge, on that far distant shore across the lake, as he steadily paddles toward it now, still a very long way away.

No Love's a Love

No love's a love without a lie
that bores deep within the sweetest fruit.
There's more abundance found in lies
than there is to be found in truth.
It's partly the bitter that makes the sweet,
the summer breeze that brings the cold
from stifling heat.
Beg pardon of me and the seasons then
which easily turn in the wind, a moon
that freezes, and sun that burns. Fat summer days
that turn to thin, gaunt autumn that gives way
to winter's starving stingy wind,
only then to spring and blossom, the sweetest fruit
of all that's love again, and all that's truth.

LONG MINNESOTA GOODBYE

They stand on the front porch at dusk, for what seems
like a lifetime, bidding each other fond, heartfelt farewells
of the classic, long Minnesota goodbye. Maybe they were
the last relatives to leave a high school graduation party
or a fortieth wedding anniversary or a grandchild's golden
birthday. You could go to the airport, fly to Chicago,
have dinner at the famous Blackhawk Restaurant, stay
overnight, fly back the next day, and they still would be
there standing on the porch, these same relatives, still
saying their long Minnesota goodbyes. In fact, you could
go away for the next twenty years, fall in love and have
a bunch of kids, watch them grow up and go out into
the world and start lives of their own, or you could get
hired and fired from three, four, or even five different
jobs, accrue and then lose a vast fortune, get divorced and
remarried several times, come back old and gray, walking
with the aid of a cane, and yes, they'd still be there, those
same relatives on that same porch, the car they drove
there still idling in the driveway, still giving each other
one more kiss and just one more hug. And, you think, my
God, when was it they started saying their goodbyes, it
was years ago, and now you can't even remember, you've
gotten so old. But they still can't seem to leave and
linger on that porch for just a little while more, saying
their long Minnesota goodbyes over and over without
end as the season slowly changes from hot to cold and
the winter winds begin to blow, and yet they can't seem
to just get into their car and go, as we only watch and
wonder why they can't bear to say their goodbyes. As
they stand on the porch at dusk, for what seems like an
eternity now, still slowly waving goodbye to us.

First Flour of Spring

Sugar snow
Brushes and
Dusts
A cold dark bark
Of the tree—
And there rose
The first
Confectionary
Flour
of spring
It flecks
And frosts its
White
Sweet
Coating
For those
all knowing
What thick
warm sap
Lies just
underneath,
Silently
Flowing

My Home's in St Peter (And Not on the Delta)

St Peter will never have a blues song immortalizing it and
I think that's a bit of a tragedy. Just take the lines from the
famous song about K.C.:

> *I'm going to Kansas City*
> *Kansas City here I come*
> *They got some crazy lil' women there*
> *And I'm gunna get me one*

Or Blind Lemon Jefferson's classic about going to Dallas:

> *Gonna take my razor and gun*
> *Cause there's so much shit in Dallas*
> *Lord I'm bound to step in some*

Or the penultimate tribute to a town or city by the legendary
Robert Johnson when he crooned and pleaded:

> *Oh baby don't you want to go*
> *Back to the land of California*
> *Or my sweet home Chicago?*

No blues great has ever felt the urge to write anything about
some small lonely southern Minnesota River town, about its
wicked, dangerous streets, its famous dens of iniquity, or even
about it boasting the biggest and finest looking gals around.
Given no blues great has ever been to St Peter that is until
about two years ago when the legendary Delta blues singer
Honeyboy Edwards somehow miraculously appeared at our
local Rock Bend Folk Festival. He was plus-90 years old then
and still going strong, but after the great stellar performance
he gave, he quickly packed up and was gone. And if the real

truth were to be told, it was most likely just another gig
for him (counted as only one in a million or so) that he's
done over the course of his long lifetime before moving
to the next one somewhere down the road. But wouldn't
it have been great for him to take one of those old blues
classics and spontaneously extemporized on where he was
at that very moment in time, right on our very own stage,
singing:

> *My home's in St Peter*
> *Way out on that old Dodd's Road*
> *I'm leavin' Chicago*
> *And peoples I sho' do hate to go*
> *I'm leavin' in the morning*
> *And lord won't be back there no mo'*

As then I can imagine faintly hearing the regular patrons
of some far-flung smoky funky Blues joint on the South
Side of Chicago suddenly giggle and wonder as they then
turned and shouted way up north this way to Honeyboy
still singing up there on stage, "Hey Honey, Where the
hell did you say St Peter was anyway!"

ELLINGTONIA

"The Jazz Impeccable"
– Ruth Stone

1.

This is no country for old white men,
Nor those faux jungle settings at the
Famous 1920s jim crow Cotton Club in
the middle of black Harlem, but maybe
a Hollywood movie set of a 1930s
screwball comedy that's not so square
or so corny or full of super-duper rich
white people, but a whole cast including
the lead stars, of all black faces, beautiful
and sophisticated, the epitome of style
removing the mask even when not asked
to reveal their true black smiles, the good
black guys win and get the sable beauty in
the end, singing "Happy Trails" again, not hardly,
nor whistling to the tune of "Dixie" but singing
a lovely duet of "Come Sunday" straight
from Duke's own *Black, Brown, and Beige* fantasy.

2.

In the beginning, God was compassionate,
merciful, never wrathful, vengeful or mean.
And it's a fact, look it up, God was a she, and
not only that, it also turns out that she was
Black and the first word ever heard from her
was "It's too dark up in here, pull them shades
up and let some light and air into this room, and
don't give me none of your looks of doom and gloom,

just lift up your voices and sing because all
God's chillun got wings!" And so the Lord saith, "It
Don't Mean a Thing (If It Ain't Got That Swing)."
And her word came to be heard through all
heaven and earth, with all of God's most beloved
creatures and all living things everywhere,
And thus, her word flourished.

3.

In the deep south resides the great unanswered
Shakespearian question, once posed by Hamlet,
the then Prince of Denmark, North Carolina, himself,
and that was, "To be or not to be," but which all God's
chillun who had wings revised and then improvised
That question when they'd sing, "Lord, ain't nothin'
but cotton as far as ma' eye can see, but
strange, *this* question keeps comin back to me,
which is, 'What does Africa really mean to me?'
from New Orleans up the Mississippi, from Clarksdale,
to Memphis, Tennessee, through all this time,
It's been heavy on my mind, and Lord, won't hardly
let me be, which ain't necessarily, 'To be or not to be,'
But Lord, after picking all this man's cotton, I still
got to ask myself, 'What does Africa mean to me?'"

4.

And thus, it came to pass, all life on earth
Rose up from a jet-black "Harlem Air-Shaft"
and came forth somewhere on 125th Street
way up North. So tired of being so downhearted,
beaten and broke, all God's chillun who had
wings then just caught the first thing smokin'
north to where it was all 'Satin Dolls' and

'Sophisticated Ladies' and where all God's
chillun who had their wings, could freely
sing God's own words, "It Don't Mean a Thing
(If It Ain't Got That Swing)." It mattered not how
far north they were, they were still all members
of that band, always headed for the promised
land, leaving a trail of a deep "Mood Indigo"
when they ran out of the goddamned South
as fast as their feet could go, all the time singing
"I'm Just a Lucky So-and-So." The most prophetic
voices in American history, it's a fact, as they all got hat,
they shouted back, "Do Nothin' Till You Hear from Me."
So by the millions they came, most if not all
'Taking the "A" Train,' men, women, very small
children, all shouted at the conductor to
"Drop Me Off in Harlem." Thus, almost the entire
African-American race got dropped right out
In front of "Duke's Place." White people back then
thought this all quite odd, but so it was and so it shall be,
For this was the word of God.

     5.

"Ko-Ko," "Perdido," "Body and Soul," no separate drinking
fountains, no black and white restrooms,
No KKK nightriders, no jim crow, only fine
custom-tailored hound's-tooth tweed jackets,
silk ties, wide brim wool felt hats as Duke
comes stepping out of a "Springtime In Africa" with a smile
so grand and so regal like the first African prince to step
off the boat, 'A Hundred (I-Have-A) Dreams Ago,' softly
humming "Cotton Tail" or even "The Beautiful
American," and as always with the Duke,
The Jazz impeccable!

6.

Here in Ellingtonia our scared democracy
was never based on a racist, murderous
Manifest Destiny. The always bright future of
Ellington Country is never short of love, charity,
compassion or mercy. The capital of Ellingtonia
lies hidden deep in this lush, green and warm
valley. And under the capitol's dome stands
none other than Louis Armstrong, the first
discoverer of the "New World A-Comin'" playing
not the "Star-Spangled Banner" or "My Old
Kentucky Home" but the "S.O.L. Blues" in his "Solitude."
News that always stays news right here in America,
played by Louie, of course, in "A Mellow Tone."

7.

In Ellingtonia, so-called jazz music will always
be the best argument against every form of chattel slavery,
and an eternal plea for complete emancipation and
freedom for all human beings, nothing more
and nothing less. Yet, proclaim this human, universal
truth that all God's chillun who had wings have
understood through all their sorrows and all their pain,
'The blues ain't nothing but a low down dirty shame.'
Through all of human history, you'll always find
the blues ain't nothing but a dark day marking time.
In Ellingtonia, it's the *Home to Harlem* version of
the Bible's golden rule, that says, 'Baby when you
hurt so bad, then it hurts me too!'

8.

In Ellingtonia, Sister "Mahalia" sings "Come Sunday"
which becomes the only real pathway to any true
form of democracy—so can she get a big 'Amen'
from the Amen Corner or a 'Yes, indeed!' or even
'Lord, have mercy!' When *all* God's chillun get
wings they then can sing that "Creole Love Call"
"Black, Brown, and Beige" for *all* of human
kind, *one and all*, no matter what ethnicity, sexuality,
gender, or race. In Ellingtonia, 'The "A" Train' will sooner
or later 'Drop Us All Up In Harlem'
right there in front of "Duke's Place."

9.

Oh, Ellingtonia!
In what specific culture, people or race
could we ever again find Duke's Place?
Can it be seen now from some distant satellite
drifting far, far out in outer space, sending
out signals to other galaxies, those ancient,
epic songs of ages gone, tall African tales, classic
Greek tragedy or is Ellingtonia, as Duke sometimes
said himself, just beyond category hurtling somewhere
through hyper-space, toward the very edge
of eternity, through the mists of the moon
toward a timeless sort of musical "Transblucency,"
a dim starry glow carrying that all-too-human
"Mood Indigo" always bluely shimmering on
some small turquois-blue glimmering of where
we all have been and where we all will
finally go—perhaps toward the very end or
maybe back to the very beginning of—
Ellingtonia Itself
As far as we know.

THE MUSEUM OF WHITE PEOPLE IN NORTH AMERICA

The other night I dreamt there, out
Towards the middle of South Dakota,
Somewhere, stood a large, imposing
Museum of White People in North America,
Solely dedicated to those
Who claimed to truly be of
The white race, so each great
Achievement of theirs, each
Valuable contribution to humanity
Was there permanently on display,
In a surprisingly small, compact,
Fully glass-enclosed case
Which sat right underneath
Vaulted ceilings of eight-inch thick concrete,
Housed like an ICBM in a hardened missile silo,
Kept preserved in a climate controlled room of pure marble,
Surrounded by great over-arching, Gothic cathedral walls,
Left there mostly forgotten
Among long gray granite corridors,
And deserted, empty halls.

THIS LITTLE LIGHT OF OURS

For RLR

This little light of ours
has become a child we two
have begat
coupled from deep within us
one to the other
We too as life-long lovers
go from night to day
and then go from day to night
turning and burning
and making this light
back and forth
from season to season
turn all our time to our reasons
Year after year
from laughter to tears
we never waver, never fear,
until it's all made perfectly clear
until this light is fully grown
and finally, we let it out
of its home, perhaps, to shine down
on some other place, all on its own.

THE MOUNTAINS OF MANKATO

Driving to Mankato
In the rain on Highway 169
On a gray, cool early fall evening,
A little before suppertime,
When we reach Seven-Mile Creek,
Renée looks up from the wheel
At the high river bluffs rising up overhead,
Just starting to turn their dark autumnal
Colors, right up their steep inclines
And down, colored bright oranges,
Reds, yellows, and browns, as she
Notes the delicate white puffs of
Damp misty smoke rising up from
The very tops of the highest bluffs,
And says that these hills could be
Steep mountains winding through
Our very own Minnesota River Valley
Rather than just pint sized, puny mole hills,
Soft sandy bluffs, and suddenly, I too, could
See them standing right there well enough
As I gazed up at those towering heights now
Reaching even higher, they seemed, somehow,
Like steep mountains with great snowy spires,
Rising way above the clouds, higher and higher,
As if they suddenly appeared just for us,
Right out of these smoky white, misty puffs,
Looming high overhead, they loom clear enough
For us to see, still looking out as we drove south,
our only wish was to just let these mountains be.

THE "NAT SHEL" TRUTH

I'll choose the blues
win or lose
get to the root
and dig the dirt
for what it's worth
instead of glory
I'll just tell my story
instead of a
pretty flower
that stands for
all those earthly powers.
I'll pay my dues
I'll sing these blues
dig down deep in the dirt
right here on earth
win or lose this is what I choose
which isn't real pretty
and could get downright shitty
but that just be the blues
that gets to the root
that's sure still to be
low-down and dirty,
and nothing but the
"Nat shel" truth.

About the Author

Philip S. Bryant, a native of Chicago, is the author of three pervious collections of poetry—*Blue Island, Sermon on a Perfect Spring Day,* and *Stompin' at the Grand Terrace: a jazz memoir in verse,* with music by Carolyn Wilkins. His work has appeared in *Blues Vision: African American Writing from Minnesota; Good Poems, American Places,* selected and introduced by Garrison Keillor; and *Where One Voice Ends Another Begins: 150 Years of Minnesota Poetry. Sermon on a Perfect Spring Day* was nominated for a Forward Prize and was a finalist for the Minnesota Book Award in Poetry. Selections from *Stompin' at the Grand Terrace* were chosen by Los Angeles Times Music Critic Ann Powers to appear in *Best Music Writing, 2010.* He was a fellow of the Minnesota State Arts Board in 1992 and 1998, and has served on the governing board of the Loft, the premier literary arts center in the Twin Cities. He has worked with the Givens Foundation as a mentor for emerging Minnesota African American writers. He was a radio-essayist for Minnesota Public Radio and is currently professor of English at Gustavus Adolphus College. He lives with his wife, Renée, in St Peter, Minnesota.